SUPER
LATERAL
THINKING
PUZZLES

Paul Sloane & Des MacHale

Illustrated by Myron Miller

Sterling Publishing Co., Inc.
New York

Edited by Peter Gordon

Library of Congress Cataloging-in-Publication Data Available

10 9 8 7 6 5 4 3 2 1

Published by Sterling Publishing Company, Inc.
387 Park Avenue South, New York, N.Y. 10016
© 2000 by Paul Sloane and Des MacHale
Distributed in Canada by Sterling Publishing
C/o Canadian Manda Group, One Atlantic Avenue, Suite 105
Toronto, Ontario, Canada M6K 3E7
Distributed in Great Britain and Europe by Cassell PLC
Wellington House, 125 Strand, London WC2R 0BB, England
Distributed in Australia by Capricorn Link (Australia) Pty Ltd.
P.O. Box 6651, Baulkham Hills, Business Centre, NSW 2153, Australia

Sterling ISBN 0-8069-4470-6

Acknowledgments

We would like to acknowledge the contribution of puzzle fans from all around the world (including many visitors to www.lateralpuzzles.com) who have encouraged and helped us. In particular we would like to thank Peter Bloxsom for "Down Periscope" and Micheal O'Fiachra for "Shoe Shop Shuffle." Ann Sloane, Hannah Sloane, and Natasha Rawdon-Jones helped edit the book and vet the clues.

CONTENTS

INTRODUCTION

A man was held in a high-security prison and closely watched. His wife sent him a letter in which she asked, "Should I plant the potatoes in the garden now?" He replied, "Do not plant anything in the garden. That is where I hid the guns." A little later he received another letter from his wife saying, "Many policemen came to our house. They dug up the whole garden but they did not find anything." He wrote back, "Now is the time to plant the potatoes."

That man used a little lateral thinking to solve his wife's gardening problem—and so can we all. We need new and creative ways of problem-solving, and more and more people see lateral thinking puzzles as a way to fire up this process. Trainers use these puzzles in management training courses to force managers to check their assumptions; teachers use them in class to stimulate and reward children; parents use them on long journeys to amuse and challenge the family. In all cases, the procedure is similar. One person knows the answer and he or she answers questions from the other players. The questions can be answered with "Yes," "No," or "Irrelevant."

These new puzzles are in sections North, South, East, and West. Is this to reflect their worldwide appeal? No—it is to emphasize that you have to look at each situation from different directions to help you solve it!

So check your assumptions, ask good questions, use your imagination, think differently, and have fun solving these puzzles!

THE PUZZLES

North Puzzles

The Deadly Sculpture
··

A penniless sculptor made a beautiful metal statue, which he sold. Because of this he died soon afterward. Why?

Clues: 57/Answer: 79.

Peak Performance
··

The body of a climber is found many years after his death a thousand feet below the summit of one of the world's highest mountains. In his pocket is a diary claiming that he had reached the summit and was on his way down. How was it discovered that he was not telling the truth?

Clues: 66/Answer: 85.

The Fatal Fish

A man was preparing a fish to eat for a meal when he made a mistake. He then knew that he would shortly die. How?

Clues: 60/Answer: 80.

Adam Had None

Adam had none. Eve had two. Everyone nowadays has three. What are they?

Clues: 54/Answer: 77.

Shot Dead

A woman who was in a house saw a stranger walking down the road. She took a gun and shot him dead. The next day she did the same thing to another stranger. Other people saw her do it and knew that she had killed the two men, yet she was never arrested or charged. Why not?

Clues: 70/Answer: 87.

Would You Believe It?

Three people were holding identical blocks of wood. They released the blocks at the same time. The blocks of wood were not attached to anything. The first person's block fell downward. The second person's block rose up. The third person's block stayed where it was, unsupported. What was going on?

Clues: 75/Answer: 91.

Jailbreak

A man planned his escape from prison very carefully. He could have carried it out in the dead of night but he preferred to do it in the middle of the morning. Why?

Clues: 62/Answer: 82.

Sitting Ducks

Why does a woman with no interest in hunting buy a gun for shooting ducks?

Clues: 70/Answer: 88.

Bald Facts

Mary, Queen of Scots was almost totally bald, and wore a wig to conceal this fact from her subjects. How was her secret revealed?

Clues: 55/Answer: 78.

Lethal Action

Brazilian authorities took actions to protect their fruit crops, and ten people from another continent died. How?

Clues: 63/Answer: 83.

Recognition

John lived in England all his life, until his parents died. He then went to Australia to visit relatives. His Aunt Mary had left England before he was born and had never returned. He had never met his Aunt Mary, had never spoken to her, and had never seen a picture of her. Yet he recognized her immediately in a crowded airport. How?

Clues: 68/Answer: 86.

Destruction

Commercial premises are destroyed by a customer. Afterward he disappears, but even if he had been caught he could not have been charged. Why?

Clues: 58/Answer: 79.

Wonderful Walk

A man and his dog went for a walk in the woods. When he returned home he invented something now worth millions of dollars. What was it?

Clues: 74/Answer: 90.

Pesky Escalator

A foreign visitor to London wanted to ride up the escalator at the subway station, but did not do so. Why?

Clues: 66/Answer: 85.

Poles Apart

How did early explorers economize with provisions for a polar expedition?

Clues: 66/Answer: 85.

Arrested Development

A bank robber grabbed several thousand dollars from a bank counter and, although he was armed, he was captured within a few seconds before he could leave the bank. How?

Clues: 54/Answer: 77.

Holed Out

A golfer dreamed all his life of getting a hole in one. However, when he eventually did get a hole in one, he was very unhappy and, in fact, quit golf altogether. Why?

Clues: 61/Answer: 82.

Trunk-ated

The police stop a car and they suspect that the trunk contains evidence linking the driver with a serious crime. However, they do not have a search warrant and if they open the trunk forcibly without probable cause, any evidence uncovered will not be admissible in court. How do they proceed?

Clues: 72/Answer: 89.

Sports Mad

Why was a keen sports fan rushing around his house looking for a roll of sticky tape?

Clues: 71/Answer: 88.

Appendectomy I & II

(There are two different solutions to this puzzle. Try both before looking at the answer to either.)

Why did a surgeon remove a perfectly healthy appendix?

Clues: 54/Answers: 77.

Riotous Assembly

After riots in a large institution, one section did not reopen for a long time after the other sections. Why?

Clues: 68–69/Answer: 86.

Kneed to Know

A woman places her hand on her husband's knee for an hour and then takes it off for ten minutes; then she places her hand on her husband's knee for another hour. Why?

Clues: 62/Answer: 82.

Bad Trip

An anti-drug agency distributed material to children in school. However, this had the opposite effect to what was intended. Why?

Clues: 54–55/Answer: 77.

Wally Test I

From the World Association of Learning, Laughter, and Youth (WALLY) comes the WALLY Test! It is a set of quick-fire questions. They may look easy, but be warned—they are designed to trick you. Write down your answers on a piece of paper and then see how many you got right. The time limit is three minutes.

1. When you see geese flying in a V formation, why is it that one leg of the V is always longer than the other?
2. Why are there so many Smiths in the telephone directory?
3. What is E.T. short for?
4. Where do you find a no-legged dog?
5. Approximately how many house bricks does it take to complete a brick house in England?
6. How do you stop a bull from charging?
7. What cheese is made backward?
8. Take away my first letter; I remain the same. Now take away my fourth letter; I remain the same. Now take away my last letter; I remain the same. What am I?
9. If a white man threw a black stone into the Red Sea, what would it become?
10. How do you make a bandstand?

Answers on page 92.

South Puzzles

Two Letters

....

Why did a man write the same two letters over and over again on a piece of paper?

Clues: 73/Answer: 89.

Body of Evidence

....

A woman goes into a police station and destroys vital evidence relating to a serious crime, yet she walks away scot-free. How come?

Clues: 55/Answer: 78.

Shakespeare's Blunder

....

What major scientific blunder did Shakespeare include in his play *Twelfth Night*?

Clues: 69/Answer: 87.

No Charge

....

A man guilty of a serious crime was arrested. The police had clear evidence against him, but he was set free without charge. Why?

Clues: 65/Answer: 84.

Pond Life

Why did the fashion for silk hats in the U.S. lead to a positive environmental increase in the number of small lakes and bogs?

Clues: 67/Answer: 85.

Shoe Shop Shuffle

In a small town there are four shoe shops of about the same size, each carrying more or less the same line in shoes. Yet one shop loses three times as many shoes to theft as each of the other shops. Why?

Clues: 70/Answer: 87.

Caesar's Blunder

Julius Caesar unexpectedly lost many of his ships when he invaded Britain. Why?

Clues: 56/Answer: 78.

Slow Death

The ancient Greek playwright Aeschylus was killed by a tortoise. How?

Clues: 71/Answer: 88.

Driving Away

A man steals a very expensive car owned by a very rich woman. Although he was a very good driver, within a few minutes he was involved in a serious accident. Why?

Clues: 58/Answer: 80.

Lit Too Well?

Local government authorities in Sussex, England, installed many more lights than were needed. This resulted in considerable damage, but the authorities were pleased with the results. Why?

Clues: 63/Answer: 83.

Quick on the Draw

Every Saturday night, the national lottery is drawn with a multimillion-dollar first prize. A man sat down in front of his TV on Saturday night and saw that the numbers drawn exactly matched the numbers on his ticket for that day's lottery. He was thrilled but did not win a penny. Why not?

Clues: 68/Answer: 86.

Scaled Down

A butcher tried to deceive a customer by pressing down on the scale while weighing a turkey to make it appear heavier than it was. But the customer's subsequent order forced the butcher to admit his deception. How?

Clues: 69/Answer: 87.

The Happy Woman

A woman going on a journey used a driver. Then she stopped and used a club to hit a large bird. She was very pleased. Why?

Clues: 61/Answer: 81.

Vandal Scandal

The authorities in Athens were very concerned that tourists sometimes hacked pieces of marble from the columns of the ancient Parthenon buildings. The practice was illegal, but some people seemed determined to take away souvenirs. How did the authorities stop this vandalism?

Clues: 73/Answer: 90.

The Deadly Drawing

A woman walked into a room and saw a new picture there. She immediately knew that someone had been killed. How?

Clues: 57/Answer: 79.

Leonardo's Secret

Leonardo da Vinci created some secret designs for his paintings that he did not want anyone to see. He hid them, but they were recently discovered. How?

Clues: 63/Answer: 82–83.

Down Periscope

A normal submarine was on the surface of the sea with its hatches open. It sailed due east for two miles. Then it stopped and went down 30 feet. It then sailed another half mile before going down a further 30 feet. All this time it kept its hatches fully open. The crew survived and were not alarmed in any way. What was going on?

Clues: 58/Answer: 79.

REALLY, CAPTAIN, THERE'S NOTHING TO WORRY ABOUT.

The Letter Left Out

For mathematical reasons, in codes and ciphers it is desirable to have 25 (which is a perfect square) letters rather than the usual 26. Which letter of the English alphabet is left out and why?

Clues: 63/Answer: 83.

Arrested Development—Again

••

Two masked men robbed a bank, but they were very quickly picked up by the police. Why?

Clues: 54/Answer: 77.

Titanic Proportions

••

How did the sinking of the *Titanic* lead directly to the sinking of another ship?

Clues: 72/Answer: 89.

The Mover

What can go from there to here by disappearing and then go from here to there by appearing?

Clues: 64/Answer: 84.

Death of a Player

A sportsman was rushed to a hospital from where he was playing and died shortly afterward. Why?

Clues: 57/Answer: 79.

Hot Picture

A woman paid an artist a large sum to create a picture, and she was very pleased with the results. Yet within a week, under her instructions, the picture was burned. Why?

Clues: 62/Answer: 82.

Genuine Article

A new play by Shakespeare is discovered. How did the literary experts prove it was authentic?

Clues: 60/Answer: 81.

Unhealthy Lifestyle

A man and a woman were exploring in the jungle. The woman had a very healthy lifestyle, while the man had a very unhealthy one. At the end of the exploration the woman died suddenly, but the man lived. Why?

Clues: 73/Answer: 89.

New World Record

A 102-year-old woman was infirm and inactive, yet one day she was congratulated on setting a new world record. What was it?

Clues: 64–65/Answer: 84.

East Puzzles

Death by Romance

A newly married couple had a fireside supper together. They were so cozy and comfortable that they dozed off on the floor. Next morning they were both found dead where they lay. What had happened?

Clues: 57/Answer: 79.

Penalty

After a World Cup soccer match, two players swapped jerseys. The police immediately arrested them. Why?

Clues: 66/Answer: 85.

Golf Challenge I, II & III

(There are three different solutions to this puzzle. Try all three before looking at any of the answers.)

A man and a woman, who were both poor golfers, challenged each other to a match. The man scored 96 while the woman scored 98. However, the woman was declared the winner. Why?

Clues: 61/Answers: 81.

Poor Investment

A man bought a house for $1,000,000 as an investment. The house was well kept and carefully maintained by a good caretaker. Although the house remained in perfect structural order, within a few years it was worthless. Why?

Clues: 67/Answer: 86.

Give Us a Hand ...

A man searching for precious stones didn't find any, but found a severed human hand instead. What had happened?

Clues: 60/Answer: 81.

Evil Intent

A rich man meets a lady at the theater and invites her back to his house for a drink. She has a drink and then leaves. About an hour later he suddenly realizes that she intends to return and burgle his house. How does he know?

Clues: 59/Answer: 80.

Two Heads Are Better Than One!

Several Americans reported they saw a creature that had two heads, two arms, and four legs. They were surprised, frightened, and alarmed, and when they told their friends, nobody believed them. But they were reliable witnesses. What had they seen?

Clues: 73/Answer: 89.

Stone Me!

A boy flung a stone at a man and many people's lives were saved. How come?

Clues: 71/Answer: 88.

Judge for Yourself

The defendant in a major lawsuit asked his lawyer if he should send the judge a box of fine cigars in the hope of influencing him. The lawyer said it was a very bad idea and would prejudice the judge against him. The defendant listened carefully, sent the cigars, and won the case. What happened?

Clues: 62/Answer: 82.

Love Letters

Why did a woman send out 1,000 anonymous Valentine's cards to different men?

Clues: 63/Answer: 83.

Strange Behavior

A man was driving down the road into town with his family on a clear day. He saw a tree and immediately stopped the car and then reversed at high speed. Why?

Clues: 71/Answer: 88.

Tree Trouble

••

The authorities were concerned that a famous old tree was being damaged because so many tourists came up to it and touched it. So a wall was built around the tree to protect it. But this had the opposite effect of that intended. Why?

Clues: 72/Answer: 89.

The Burial Chamber

••

Why did a man build a beautiful burial chamber, complete with sculptures and paintings, and then deliberately wreck it?

Clues: 55/Answer: 78.

Miscarriage of Justice

An Italian judge released a guilty man and convicted an innocent man and as a result the confectionery industry has greatly benefited. Why?

Clues: 64/Answer: 84.

Offenses Down

The police in Sussex, England, found a new way to complete their form-filling and paperwork that significantly reduced crime. What was it?

Clues: 65/Answer: 84.

Police Chase

A high-speed police car chases a much slower vehicle in which criminals are escaping. But the police fail to catch them. Why?

Clues: 67/Answer: 85.

Café Society

A mall café is pestered by teenagers who come in, buy a single cup of coffee, and stay for hours, and thus cut down on available space for other customers. How does the owner get rid of them, quite legally?

Clues: 56/Answer: 78.

Hi, Jean!

....

A shop owner introduced expensive new procedures to make his premises more hygienic, but the results were the very opposite. Why?

Clues: 61/Answer: 82.

The Empty Machine

....

A gumball machine dispensed gum when quarters were inserted. When the machine was opened, there was no money inside. A considerable number of gumballs had been consumed and the machine did not appear to have been interfered with in any way. What had happened?

Clues: 59/Answer: 80.

Take a Fence

A man painted his garden fence green and then went on holiday. When he came back two weeks later, he was amazed to see that the fence was blue. Nobody had touched the fence. What had happened?

Clues: 72/Answer: 88.

Wally Test II

Time for another WALLY Test. The questions may look easy, but be warned—they're designed to trip you up. Write down your answers on a piece of paper and then see how many you got right. The time limit is three minutes.

1. What should you give an injured lemon?
2. If an atheist died in church, what would they put on his coffin?
3. Who went into the lion's den unarmed and came out alive?
4. A man rode down the street on a horse, yet walked. How come?
5. How can you eat an egg without breaking the shell?
6. Why was King Henry VIII buried in Westminster Abbey?
7. In China they hang many criminals, but they will not hang a man with a wooden leg. Why?
8. Why do storks stand on one leg?
9. A circular field is covered in thick snow. A black cow with white spots is in the middle. Two white cows with black spots are on the edge of the field. What time is it?
10. What was the problem with the wooden car with wooden wheels and a wooden engine?

Answers on page 92.

West Puzzles

Sex Discrimination

••

When lawyers went to prison to visit their clients they found that female lawyers were searched on entry but male lawyers were not. Why?

Clues: 69/Answer: 87.

Weight Loss

••

How did a Japanese diet clinic achieve great weight-loss results for its patients even though they did not change their diet or undertake more activity than normal?

Clues: 74/Answer: 90.

Psychic

You enter a parking lot and see a woman walking toward you. You then see a row of cars and know immediately which one is hers. How?

Clues: 68/Answer: 86.

The Happy Robber

A robber holds up a bank, but leaves with no money whatsoever. However, he is more pleased than if he had left with lots of money. Why?

Clues: 61/Answer: 81.

Siege Mentality

A city is under siege. The attackers have run out of ammunition and have suffered heavy casualties. Yet they take the city within a few days without further losses. How?

Clues: 70/Answer: 87.

Carrier Bags

During World War II, the British Royal Navy had very few aircraft carriers. What ingenious plan was devised to remedy this deficiency?

Clues: 56/Answer: 78.

The Cathedral Untouched

When London was bombed during World War II, St. Paul's Cathedral, in the center of the city, was never hit. Why not?

Clues: 56/Answer: 78–79.

Bags Away

An airplane nearly crashed because one of the passengers had not fastened his suitcase securely enough. What happened?

Clues: 55/Answer: 77.

The Sad Samaritan

Jim saw a stranded motorist on a country road. The motorist had run out of fuel, so Jim took him to the nearest garage and then drove him back to his car. Jim felt good that he had been such a good Samaritan, but discovered something later that made him very sad. What was it?

Clues: 69/Answer: 87.

The Tallest Tree

Men found what they suspected was the tallest tree in Australia. It was growing in the outback in rough terrain and with other trees around. They did not have any advanced instruments with them. How did they accurately measure the height of the tree?

Clues: 72/Answer: 88.

The Unwelcome Guest

A couple had a neighbor who continually arrived at mealtimes in the hope of getting a free meal. How did they use their very friendly dog to persuade the neighbor not to come for free meals again?

Clues: 73/Answer: 89–90.

Poor Show

Every time he performed in public, it was a complete flop. Yet he became famous for it, and won medals and prizes. People came from all over and paid to see him perform. Who was he?

Clues: 67/Answer: 86.

Message Received

How did Alexander the Great send secret messages with his envoy?

Clues: 64/Answer: 83.

The Mighty Stone

There was a huge boulder in the middle of a village green. It was too big to be moved, too hard to split, and dynamiting it was too dangerous. How did a simple peasant suggest getting rid of it?

Clues: 64/Answer: 84.

The World's Most Expensive Car

The most expensive car ever made is for sale. Although many people want to own it and can afford to buy it, nobody will do so. Why?

Clues: 75/Answer: 91.

The Fatal Fall

A woman dropped a piece of wood. She picked it up again and carried on as if nothing had happened. The wood was not damaged and she was not injured, but the incident cost her her life. Why?

Clues: 59/Answer: 80.

Election Selection

There is an election in a deprived city area. All the political parties put up candidates, actively canvass, and spend money on their campaigns. Yet the election is won by a candidate who did not canvass or advertise and is unknown to all of the electors. How?

Clues: 58–59/Answer: 80.

Well Trained

A man, a woman, and a child are watching a train come into a station. "Here it comes," says the man. "Here she comes," says the woman. "Here he comes," says the child. Who was correct?

Clues: 74/Answer: 90.

Razor Attack

A man had his throat attacked by a woman with a razor, yet he suffered no serious injuries. How come?

Clues: 68/Answer: 86.

The Old Crooner

How did Bing Crosby reduce the crime rate in various U.S. cities?

Clues: 65/Answer: 84–85.

Generosity?

A man took considerable trouble to acquire some money, but then quickly gave most of it away. Why?

Clues: 60/Answer: 81.

The Parson's Pup

Why did the vicar want only a black dog?

Clues: 65/Answer: 85.

Watch That Man!

A runner was awarded a prize for winning a marathon. But the judges disqualified him when they saw a picture of his wristwatch. Why?

Clues: 74/Answer: 90.

THE CLUES

Adam Had None

It has nothing to do with family, relations, bones, or physical appearance.

It has to do with names.

Appendectomy I & II

No financial gain is involved in either solution.

The doctors who removed the healthy appendixes acted out of good motives.

Both solutions involve situations in the first part of the 20th century.

Arrested Development

The robber wanted to get out of the bank as quickly as he could.

There was nothing particularly noticeable or remarkable about the bank robber that would make him easy to identify.

He was not very bright.

Arrested Development—Again

The robbers wore masks so as not to be recognized.

They made a clean getaway.

Bank employees noticed something about the two men.

The men were brothers.

Bad Trip

The anti-drug agency wanted to actively promote a message that drugs were bad, but inadvertently they ended up promoting the opposite message.

The agency distributed pencils to children and the children used them.

Bags Away

The passenger's suitcase was stored in the hold of the plane.

He was not a terrorist or criminal.

The passenger's suitcase did not contain chemicals, explosives, or drugs.

Bald Facts

Mary, Queen of Scots took great care never to be seen without her wig.

Her wig was very good and looked completely natural.

Although Mary, Queen of Scots never wanted to be seen without her wig, she was not upset or embarrassed when it eventually happened, even though many people saw it.

Body of Evidence

The woman was seen entering and leaving the police station, but no one tried to stop her.

She was not a criminal or deliberately aiding a criminal.

She was doing her job.

The Burial Chamber

The burial chamber wasn't built for use by the builder.

He wrecked it before anyone was buried there.

He did not wreck it out of spite or anger. He deliberately destroyed it in order to deceive.

He wrecked the chamber in order to save the chamber.

Caesar's Blunder

The sea was calm and there were no storms when Caesar sailed across the channel and arrived in Britain.

He arrived safely and disembarked his troops and equipment.

Caesar had never visited Britain before.

He had learned to sail in the Mediterranean.

Café Society

The café owner did not change the menu or prices or music in the café.

He changed the appearance of the café in a way that embarrassed the teenagers.

Carrier Bags

The suggestion was a way of creating new aircraft carriers much more cheaply than by the conventional methods.

It would possibly have been practical in the North Atlantic.

They were disposable carriers.

The Cathedral Untouched

The area all around St. Paul's was heavily bombed, but it appeared that no bombs could fall on St. Paul's.

The German bombers deliberately avoided bombing it.

They were not acting out of any religious or moral principles.

The Deadly Drawing

She was correct in her deduction that someone had been killed.

She did not know the person who had been killed, nor who had killed them, nor how they had died.

She had never been in that room before and she had not seen the picture before.

The Deadly Sculpture

He lived a lonely life in a remote building.

He made the statue out of copper. It was taken far away and he never saw it again.

He died as the result of an accident. No other person or animal or sculpture was involved.

Death by Romance

They did not die of food or gas poisoning, nor from the effects of any kind of exertion.

They were not murdered. They died by accident.

They were in an unusual house.

Death of a Player

The man was not involved in any collisions or tackles and did not suffer any injuries, yet it was because of his sport that he accidentally died.

He was a golfer, but he was not hit by a club or a ball or indeed by anything.

If only he had put his tee in his pocket!

Destruction

The customer was a man who accidentally destroyed the premises without knowing that he was doing so.

He was there the whole time that the premises were being destroyed.

He was very overweight.

Down Periscope

The submarine was in water at all times and was not on dry ground or in dry dock.

No water entered the submarine.

This could happen only in certain places, and not in the open sea.

Driving Away

Driving conditions were excellent, but the thief found the woman's car very difficult to drive.

She had had the car modified.

The rich woman suffered from some of the same frailties as other old people.

There was nothing unusual about the car's engine, gears, wheels, steering, or bodywork.

Election Selection

The successful candidate had no particular experience, qualifications, or characteristics that qualified him for the job or increased his appeal to voters.

He did not canvass or advertise or spend money in any way to influence the voters, and he remained unknown to the voters.

The other candidates were competent and trustworthy and did nothing to disqualify themselves.

He changed something about himself.

The Empty Machine

Kids had cheated the gum company.

They had not put quarters into the machine, but they had obtained gumballs.

The machine was rusty, but it still worked fine.

Evil Intent

It was nothing she said or did with the man. He did not remember anything to cause his realization that she planned to burgle him.

He noticed something.

While he was preparing the drinks, she did something.

He had his hands full.

The Fatal Fall

The woman wasn't a criminal, and no crime was involved.

She was quite upset to have dropped the piece of wood.

The wood was a cylinder about one foot long.

The piece of wood was not particularly valuable and could easily be replaced.

Many people saw her drop the piece of wood.

The Fatal Fish

The man died in an accident. He was not poisoned or stabbed.

No other person was involved. No crime was involved.

The man did not eat the fish. The type of fish is irrelevant. It was dead.

He was not indoors.

Generosity?

He had not intended to give any money away, and did not do so out of altruistic motives.

He was under pressure.

Genuine Article

The play was written by Shakespeare and this was proven beyond doubt.

It had been copied and written out on a computer, so there were no clues from the paper or handwriting.

No analysis of the style or content was needed to prove its authenticity.

Give Us a Hand ...

The man whose hand it was had also been looking for precious stones.

He had been forced to cut off his own hand.

To find these precious stones, men needed strong limbs, good eyes, good lungs, and great fitness.

Golf Challenge I, II & III

I. The woman's gender was no handicap.

II. The woman was more than a match for the man.

III. It was a very wet day and the golf course was flooded.

The Happy Robber

He was poor. He stole something from the bank, but it was not money.

He made no financial gain from the theft. He stole for love.

He stole a rare liquid.

The Happy Woman

Although she used a driver, she walked about four miles in the course of her tour.

She wore special shoes.

She saw many flags.

Hi, Jean!

The shop owner sold food and he wanted to present it in the best possible light.

He took action to deter and kill pests.

Holed Out

It was not a good shot that got him the hole in one.

He should have been more careful.

The golfer's ball rebounded into the hole.

Another person was involved.

Hot Picture

She loved the picture, but she deliberately had it burned. No trace of it was left.

There was no criminal intent on her part, and she did not make any financial gains.

The picture was a present.

Her husband was a motorcyclist.

Jailbreak

There was an advantage to him in escaping in the morning. It had nothing to do with light, or deliveries, or prison officer routines.

He did not want to be spotted once he was outside the prison.

He knew that his escape would be detected after about half an hour.

Judge for Yourself

The defendant's actions probably influenced the judge in his favor.

The judge was scrupulously honest and would resent any intent to bribe or influence him.

Kneed to Know

The man and his wife were in a room full of people.

She put her hand on his knee not as a sign of affection or encouragement but as an act of communication.

He gained an understanding through her actions.

Leonardo's Secret

Leonardo hid the designs in a place where he thought nobody would ever find them, but they were not buried or locked away.

People carefully stored the hidden designs for years without realizing they had them.

Lethal Action

The dead people were Africans. They didn't eat the fruit.

The Brazilian authorities' actions involved pesticides.

The Africans acted illegally. Their deaths were accidents.

The Letter Left Out

The letter that is left out is chosen not because it is rarely used but because it is easily substituted without any risk of misunderstanding.

Lit Too Well?

The authorities deliberately set up lights in fields and on roads even though people living there had not requested them and did not need them.

There was damage to fields, crops, roads, and farm animals as a result.

Overall, though, human lives were saved.

Love Letters

She didn't know the men and didn't like any of them.

She had malicious intentions.

There was potential financial gain for her.

Message Received

Envoys were thoroughly searched when they arrived at a foreign location to check for hidden messages.

The envoys did not memorize the messages or ever know or see the contents of the messages.

The messages were hidden on the person of the envoy but they could not be seen, even when the envoy was naked.

The Mighty Stone

The peasant did not suggest building over it.

He suggested a way of moving the stone, but not by pushing it or pulling it.

He used its own weight to help move it.

Miscarriage of Justice

The Italian judge tried a rebel, but released a robber.

The Italian was not in Italy when he made the judgment.

The judge, the rebel, and the robber never ate any chocolate.

The Mover

It is something you see every day.

In fact you have seen one in the last few seconds.

New World Record

She did not do anything physical.

She became the only known person to achieve a certain feat.

It was not her age alone that did this, though one would have to be old to do it.

No Charge

The arresting officer followed the correct procedure and read the man his rights. There was clear evidence of his crime. But his lawyer got him released on a clear breach of his rights.

The crime he committed is irrelevant.

He did not own any music CDs or radios.

Offenses Down

The police officers filled in their reports and forms in a different fashion, which reduced crime, but they did not fill them in any better or quicker or more accurately or with more information than before.

They filled in the reports by hand, not by computer.

The key difference was their location when they did the paperwork.

The Old Crooner

Bing Crosby himself did not take part in the action to reduce crime.

His songs were used to reduce crime.

His songs are old-fashioned and melodic, which means that some people like them and some do not.

The Parson's Pup

The fact that he is religious is not relevant.

The vicar is particular about his appearance.

Peak Performance

He had been dead for many years, so it was not possible to tell from his physical condition or clothing whether he had reached the summit.

The manner of his death is not relevant.

No camera was involved.

What would he have done had he reached the summit?

Penalty

It was a regular soccer match played in the World Cup in front of thousands of people.

The players were not criminals or terrorists—just soccer players.

The match was played in an Arab country.

Pesky Escalator

There was no one else around.

The foreign visitor saw a sign.

He was very obedient.

Poles Apart

The explorers knew that there would be no sources of food other than what they carried with them.

They did something that would not normally be considered a good idea.

Police Chase

The fast police car was right behind the criminals' vehicle and there was no other traffic or vehicle involved. The roads were clear and the weather was fine.

The getaway vehicle was a bus.

The bus driver was number seven.

Pond Life

The same environmental change would have occurred if felt hats or woolen hats had become very popular.

More silk hats were sold and fewer other hats were sold.

Fur hats were out of fashion.

Poor Investment

There were no other buildings nearby, and no buildings or roads were added or removed in the vicinity.

There were no earthquakes, floods, fires, or eruptions, and no damage by trees or vegetation.

The house had a beautiful view.

Poor Show

His performances were always a flop, but he was very successful.

He was not in comedy, music, cinema, or theater.

His most famous performance was in Mexico.

He was a sportsman.

Psychic

You see the cars after you see the woman, and you did not see her leaving the car.

There is something different in the appearance of her car.

She is carrying something.

Quick on the Draw

He had a perfectly valid ticket for that day's lottery, but he was not a prizewinner.

He saw the exact numbers on his ticket come up on the TV show.

He had a cruel wife.

Razor Attack

She meant to hurt him, and he did not defend himself.

The razor made full contact with his unprotected throat.

She could not have shaved him either.

Recognition

His Aunt Mary was not carrying a sign or wearing anything distinctive. She did not have any disabilities or characteristics that would make her stand out.

He had not arranged to meet her in a specific place or asked her to wear or carry anything in particular.

He recognized her from her facial appearance.

Riotous Assembly

The section did not have the equipment it needed to reopen.

The rioters had used everything they could lay their hands on.

The police had intervened but were driven back when the rioters threw rocks at them.

The Sad Samaritan

Jim was not robbed or deceived by the motorist in any way.

Jim tried his best to help, but failed.

The motorist was stranded.

Scaled Down

The butcher had only one turkey left.

He weighed it for the customer.

He pressed down on the scale with his thumb in order to give it an exaggerated weight.

Sex Discrimination

The prison guards were not acting in a discriminatory, sexist, or unfair fashion, but simply following procedures.

Women were more likely to fall afoul of the security equipment.

Shakespeare's Blunder

The blunder did not involve physics, chemistry, mathematics, or astronomy.

The blunder concerned the twins, Viola and Sebastian.

Shoe Shop Shuffle

The four shops have similar staffing, lighting, and security arrangements.

The shop that suffers the heaviest thefts is not in a worse part of town or in an environment that is more popular with criminals.

The shop that suffers the heaviest thefts does something different with its shoes.

Shot Dead

The woman and the strangers were neither criminals nor police.

The strangers did not see the woman and did not know that she was in the house.

The strangers were armed and were a threat to the woman.

Siege Mentality

This took place in the Middle Ages.

The defenders had plenty of food, water, and ammunition.

The attackers had catapulted rocks over the walls, but had now run out of ammunition.

Sitting Ducks

The woman loves animals and hates hunting. She does not intend to use the gun for hunting or for self-defense.

There is no criminal intent in mind.

The ducks are already dead when she shoots them.

Slow Death

Aeschylus did not trip over the tortoise or slip on it.

He did not eat it or attempt to eat it. He was not poisoned or bitten by the tortoise.

No other human was involved in his death.

Sports Mad

The sports fan was not exercising. He was not injured. He wanted the tape because of his sports obsession.

No sports equipment is involved.

He was a football fan. He followed his team fanatically but rarely got the chance to go to the games.

Stone Me!

The man was much bigger than the boy.

The stone hit the man on the head.

Many people watched.

Strange Behavior

There were many trees along the side of the road. The man had never seen or noticed this tree before.

There was something different about this tree.

His primary concern was safety.

The tree itself was not a threat to him.

Take a Fence

No other person or animal was involved.

The change in color was not caused by the sun or wind.

The change in color was caused by the rain, but every other house and fence in the area remained unchanged in color.

The Tallest Tree

The men did not use angles or shadows.

They did not climb the tree.

They measured it accurately using rope and measuring lines.

Titanic Proportions

The ship that sank was not involved in the sinking of the *Titanic* or the rescue operation.

Laws were passed to ensure that ships improved their safety.

One ship sank but all the passengers were saved.

Tree Trouble

The wall was successful in keeping prying people away from the tree—just as intended.

The tree died.

Trunk-ated

The policeman is able to prove that there is something suspicious in the trunk without opening it.

He suspects that there is a body in the trunk.

How do you attempt to contact a dead man?

Two Heads Are Better Than One!

They were not drunk or under any strange influence.

This happened in North America.

They had seen a creature they had never seen before.

Two Letters

He is not trying to form words or to communicate or send a message.

The man is working on a crossword puzzle.

The letters he writes are S and E.

Unhealthy Lifestyle

The man's unhealthy habits helped save him.

No other people were involved.

The woman died from poison.

The Unwelcome Guest

The neighbor liked the dog and the dog did not annoy the neighbor.

The couple gave the neighbor a fine meal.

He was horrified at what happened next.

Vandal Scandal

The authorities did not add extra security or protection for the ancient buildings.

They fooled the people who were determined to take souvenirs.

Tourists went away happy.

Watch That Man!

The wristwatch was perfectly legal and did not give the runner an unfair advantage.

The man had cheated.

The clue to his cheating was that his wristwatch had changed hands.

Weight Loss

The diet and the daily regimen were not changed. But something else about the clinic was changed, and this produced the weight loss in patients.

The change made the patients work a little harder in normal activities.

The fact that the clinic is in Japan is not particularly relevant. Similar results could have been obtained in many countries—but not in Belgium or Holland.

Well Trained

Do not take this puzzle too seriously—it involves a bad pun.

The child was correct. But why?

Wonderful Walk

Something annoying happened during the walk in the woods.

It gave the man an idea.

He invented a popular fastener.

The World's Most Expensive Car

The car was used once and is in good condition, but it has not been driven for many years.

Most people have seen it on TV, but they can't name the man who drove it.

It is not associated with any celebrity or with any remarkable historical event or tragedy, though when it was driven it was a special event at the time.

It was developed at great expense for practical use and not for show or exhibition.

Would You Believe It?

The blocks of wood were identical and so were the people (for the purposes of this puzzle), but their circumstances were not identical.

Normal forces were at work in all three cases—nothing unusual was going on.

THE ANSWERS

Adam Had None
The letter e.

Appendectomy I
The patient was a man who was going on a polar expedition in the first years of the 20th century. If he got appendicitis in such a remote region, he would die due to lack of treatment, so his healthy appendix was removed as a precaution.

Appendectomy II
Shell shock was not recognized as a genuine medical condition during World War I. Sympathetic surgeons often removed perfectly healthy appendixes from shell-shock victims so they could be sent home on medical grounds.

Arrested Development
The bank robber dashed to the revolving door and tried to push it in the direction in which it would not revolve.

Arrested Development—Again
Bank employees noticed that the two men were Siamese twins. This reduced the number of suspects dramatically.

Bad Trip
The anti-drug agency distributed pencils that had TOO COOL TO DO DRUGS printed on them. As the children sharpened the pencils down, the message became—COOL TO DO DRUGS and eventually just DO DRUGS.

Bags Away
The passenger's pet dog escaped from his suitcase in the hold and bit through some of the plane's electric cables, thereby disrupting the plane's controls.

Bald Facts
After Mary, Queen of Scots had been beheaded, the executioner held up her head to show it to the mob. The head fell out of the wig.

Body of Evidence
The woman is a cleaner who wipes the fingerprints from a murder weapon in the course of her dusting.

The Burial Chamber
The man was building the burial chamber of an Egyptian pharaoh in ancient times. He built the real burial chamber deep inside a pyramid. He also built another burial chamber that was easier to find that he deliberately wrecked so that when any future graverobbers found it, they would think that earlier graverobbers had found the tomb and taken the treasure.

Caesar's Blunder
Since the tides in the Mediterranean are very weak, Julius Caesar did not beach his ships high enough when he landed on the shores of England. Many ships floated off on the next tide and were lost.

Café Society
The café owner installed pink lighting that highlighted all the teenagers' acne!

Carrier Bags
It was seriously proposed that the British Navy tow icebergs from the north and shape the tops to serve as aircraft carriers. They could not be sunk, lasted quite a long time, and could be cheaply replaced. However, it was too lateral a solution for the Navy high command!

The Cathedral Untouched
On a moonlit night, the dome of St. Paul's cathedral acted

like a shining beacon to guide German planes during the blackout, so they deliberately avoided bombing it.

The Deadly Drawing
She entered the room and saw the chalk picture outline of a body on the floor. It was the site of a recent murder and the chalk marked the position of the body.

The Deadly Sculpture
He lived in a tower on a hill. Being poor, he had no money for materials, so he took the copper lightning rod from the building. He made a beautiful statue with the copper, but soon afterward the tower was struck by lightning and he was killed.

Death by Romance
The couple spent their honeymoon on a trip to the Arctic. They stayed in an igloo. The fire melted a hole in the roof and they died of exposure.

Death of a Player
The man was a golfer who absentmindedly sucked on his tee between shots. The tee had picked up deadly weed killer used on the golf course, and the man died from poisoning.

Destruction
The body of a very overweight man is being cremated. There is so much fat that the crematorium catches fire and is burned down.

Down Periscope
The submarine started at sea and then sailed into a canal system, where each lock dropped the water level by 30 feet.

Driving Away
The rich woman was very nearsighted, but did not like wearing glasses or contact lenses. So she had her windshield ground to her prescription. The thief could not see clearly through it.

Election Selection
The successful candidate changed his name to "None of the Above." His name appeared on the list below the other candidates (Davies, Garcia, and Jones). The voters in the deprived area resented all the established political parties and voted for None of the Above as a protest.

The Empty Machine
Kids had poured water into molds the size of quarters. The molds were placed in the deep freeze and the resulting ice coins were used in the machine. They subsequently melted and dripped out of the machine leaving no trace.

Evil Intent
The man happened to put his door key in his mouth (because he was holding lots of other things in his hands). The key tasted of soap. He deduced correctly that his visitor had taken an impression of the key in a bar of soap in order to make a duplicate key so that he could be burgled.

The Fatal Fall
The woman was running in the Olympics in her national relay team. She dropped the baton and her team ended up losing. When she later returned to her country, the tyrannical despot who ran it was so displeased that he had her shot.

The Fatal Fish
The man's boat had capsized and he was adrift in an inflatable dinghy in a cold ocean. He caught a fish and, while cutting it up, his knife slipped and punctured the dinghy.

Generosity?
The man robbed a bank and was chased on foot by the public and the police. He threw away much of the cash he had acquired, which caused some chasers to stop to pick up the money and caused a rumpus that delayed the police and allowed the criminal to escape. The people who picked up the bills were forced to give them back or face prosecution.

Genuine Article
The play was written by Brian Shakespeare, a contemporary dramatist. He vouched for its authenticity.

Give Us a Hand ...
The man was a diver searching for pearls in giant clams. A previous diver had had his hand trapped in the clam, and as his oxygen ran out the poor man was forced to cut off his own hand.

Golf Challenge I
The woman's handicap was more than two shots greater than the man's.

Golf Challenge II
They were playing match play. The woman won more holes than the man.

Golf Challenge III
They were playing darts—highest score with three darts.

The Happy Robber
The man was robbing a blood bank. He stole some rare blood that his sick daughter needed for a life-saving operation. He could not have afforded to buy the blood.

The Happy Woman
She was playing golf and hit an eagle—two under par and a very good score.

Hi, Jean!
The shop owner introduced an electric insect zapper to kill flies and other insects that might land on the food. However, when the flies were "zapped," they were propelled up to five feet, and often fell on the food.

Holed Out
The golfer's ball rebounded off the head of another golfer who was crossing the green. The ball bounced into the hole. However, the man who was hit died.

Hot Picture
The woman commissioned a tattoo artist to produce a beautiful tattoo on her husband's back as a birthday present. The picture was fine, but the next day the unfortunate man was killed in a motorcycle accident. He was cremated.

Jailbreak
The man knew that his escape would be detected after about half an hour. He escaped at 10:30 on Tuesday morning just 30 minutes before the routine weekly alarm test, when everyone in the surrounding area would ignore the siren.

Judge for Yourself
The defendant sent the judge a cheap box of cigars and included the plaintiff's name card in it!

Kneed to Know
The wife of the deaf Thomas Edison used to go with him to the theater. She drummed out on his knee in Morse code with her fingers what the actors were saying on stage.

Leonardo's Secret
Leonardo hid the secret designs by painting over them with beautiful oil paintings. He knew that no one would

remove such masterpieces. But he did not know that modern x-ray techniques would allow art historians to see through the oil paintings and reveal his designs.

Lethal Action
The Brazilian customs authorities require that all imported fruit be sprayed with pesticides to prevent insects or diseases from reaching domestic crops. They sprayed the hold of a fruit ship arriving from the Ivory Coast in Africa just before it docked in Brazil. They subsequently found the bodies of 10 stowaways who had hidden in the ship's hold and who had been poisoned by the pesticides.

The Letter Left Out
The letter W is left out because it can always be written as UU—double U!

Lit Too Well?
During the blitz in World War II, London was subjected to heavy bombing by German planes. Sussex is south of London. It is on the flight path from Germany and part of its coastline resembles the Thames estuary. The authorities put lights in fields and in empty countryside to look like blacked-out London from the air. Some German aircrews were deceived and dropped their bombs in the wrong place.

Love Letters
She was a divorce lawyer drumming up business!

Message Received
Alexander the Great had the envoy's head shaved and then the message was tattooed on the envoy's head. Then he let the man's hair grow for a few weeks. When the envoy arrived, his head was shaved to reveal the message.

The Mighty Stone
The peasant first suggested putting props around the boulder to stabilize it. Then a team of workers dug a big hole around and halfway under the boulder. When the hole was big enough, they pulled away the props and the boulder rolled into the hole where it was then covered with earth.

Miscarriage of Justice
The Italian was Pontius Pilate, who released Barabbas and condemned Jesus Christ to die by crucifixion at Easter time. Every year Easter is marked by the sale of millions of chocolate Easter eggs worldwide.

The Mover
The letter t.

New World Record
The woman's great-great-granddaughter gave birth, so the old woman became the only known great-great-great-grandmother alive. The family had six generations alive at the same time.

No Charge
The man was totally deaf, so he did not hear his rights being read to him by the arresting officer.

Offenses Down
The police officers filled in their reports and forms while sitting in marked police cars parked outside the homes of known criminals. Drug dealers, fences, and burglars found it very inhibiting and bad for business to have a marked police car outside their houses. So crime went down.

The Old Crooner
The owners of shopping malls found that if they used Bing Crosby songs for the music in the public areas, then

they had fewer undesirable youngsters hanging around and less crime was committed.

The Parson's Pup
The vicar wears black suits and knows that light-colored dog hairs will show up on his suits, but that black ones will not be noticed.

Peak Performance
In the climber's knapsack was his national flag, which he would have planted on the summit had he reached it.

Penalty
It was the women's World Cup and the match was played in a country with strict rules about female nudity or undressing in public.

Pesky Escalator
The foreign visitor saw a sign saying, "Dogs must be carried." He did not have a dog!

Poles Apart
Before the expedition the explorers deliberately ate a lot of fatty foods and put on several pounds of extra weight so that the fat would serve as food and fuel.

Police Chase
The getaway vehicle was a double-decker bus that went under a low bridge. The top deck of the bus was cut off and fell onto the pursuing police car. (This is a famous scene in a movie featuring James Bond, Agent 007.)

Pond Life
Because silk hats came into fashion, the demand for beaver hats decreased. More beavers meant more small lakes and bogs.

Poor Investment

The house was in a beautiful clifftop location. But within a few years, coastal erosion accelerated, and nothing could stop the house from eventually falling into the sea.

Poor Show

His name was Dick Fosbury, inventor of the famous Fosbury flop, a new high-jumping technique that involved going over the bar backward and that revolutionized the sport. He won the gold medal in the Mexico City Olympics in 1968.

Psychic

You notice that the woman is carrying a kettle. It is a very cold morning and only one of the cars has the windshield de-iced. You deduce correctly that she has defrosted her windshield with the kettle and is returning it to her home before setting off on her journey.

Quick on the Draw

The man's wife had played a trick on him. She called him to watch the drawing on TV and he was unaware that he was watching a video of the previous week's draw. She had bought him a ticket for today's draw and chosen the previous week's winning numbers.

Razor Attack

The woman forgot to plug in the razor!

Recognition

His Aunt Mary and his mother were identical twins.

Riotous Assembly

The institution was a university. Rioting students had raided the geology department and used rock samples as ammunition.

The Sad Samaritan
Jim found the full gas can in the trunk of his car. He had driven off and left the motorist stranded.

Scaled Down
The butcher had only one turkey left. The customer asked him its weight and he weighed it. The customer then asked if he had a slightly heavier one, so the butcher put the turkey away and then brought it out again. This time when he weighed it, he pressed down on the scale with his thumb in order to give it an exaggerated weight. The customer then said, "Fine—I'll take both!"

Sex Discrimination
It was found that the female lawyers wore underwire bras, which set off the very sensitive metal detectors.

Shakespeare's Blunder
The identical twins Viola and Sebastian are different sexes. This is impossible.

Shoe Shop Shuffle
One shop puts left shoes outside as samples; the other three shops put right shoes out. Display shoes are stolen, but the thieves have to form pairs, so more are taken from the store showing left shoes.

Shot Dead
The woman was a Russian sniper who, during the siege of Stalingrad in World War II, shot several German soldiers.

Siege Mentality
Several of the attacking soldiers had died of the plague. Their bodies were catapulted over the walls, and they infected many of the defenders, who were in a much more confined space. The defenders soon surrendered.

Sitting Ducks
The woman is an aeronautics engineer. She uses the gun to shoots ducks at airplane engines to test how they handle high-speed impacts with birds.

Slow Death
Aeschylus was killed when the tortoise was dropped on him from a height by an eagle who may have mistaken the bald head of Aeschylus for a rock on which to break the tortoise.

Sports Mad
The man wanted to record his favorite football team on TV. However, the safety tab on his only videocassette had been removed and he needed to cover the space with tape.

Stone Me!
David slew Goliath with a stone from his sling and a major battle was averted.

Strange Behavior
The man saw a tree lying across the road. He was in Africa and he knew that blocking the road with a tree was a favorite trick of armed bandits, who then waited for a car to stop at the tree so that they could ambush and rob the passengers. He guessed correctly that this was the case here, so he reversed quickly to avoid danger.

Take a Fence
The man had made green paint by mixing yellow paint and blue paint. The blue paint was oil-based, but the yellow paint was water-based. Heavy rain had dissolved the yellow paint, leaving the fence decidedly blue.

The Tallest Tree
The men chopped down the tree and then measured it on the ground!

Titanic Proportions
One of the reasons why so many perished on the *Titanic* was the shortage of lifeboats. Laws were passed to ensure that all ships had adequate lifeboats for all crew and passengers. One small ship took on so many lifeboats that it sank under their weight. (It must have been overloaded already!)

Tree Trouble
The foundation of the wall cut through the roots of the ancient tree and killed it.

Trunk-ated
A policeman suspects that there is the body of a murdered man in the trunk. He dials the cell phone of the victim and the phone is heard ringing in the trunk.

Two Heads Are Better Than One!
They were Native Americans who saw a European riding a horse. It was the first time they had seen a horse.

Two Letters
The man is given the world's most difficult crossword and offered a prize of $100 for every letter he gets right. He puts "S" for each initial letter and "E" in every other space. S is the commonest initial letter and E the commonest letter in the English language.

Unhealthy Lifestyle
The man was a heavy smoker. His smoke kept away mosquitoes and other insects. The woman died from an insect bite.

The Unwelcome Guest
The couple gave the neighbor a good meal, and when he finished, they gave his scrap-filled plate to the dog, who proceeded to lick it clean. They then put the plate straight

back into the cupboard—pretending that was their normal procedure. The neighbor did not come back for any more meals!

Vandal Scandal
The authorities arranged for some chips of marble from the same original quarry source as the Parthenon to be distributed around the site every day. Tourists thought that they had picked up a piece of the original columns and were satisfied.

Watch That Man!
A picture of the runner early in the race showed him wearing his watch on his right wrist. When he crossed the finishing line, it was on his left wrist. The judges investigated further and found that one man had run the first half of the race and his identical twin brother had run the second half. They had switched at a toilet on the route.

Weight Loss
The doctor running the clinic had noticed that people living at high altitudes were generally thin. The air is thinner and people use more energy in all activities, including breathing. He therefore located his diet clinic at 8,000 feet above sea level and the patients found that they lost weight.

Well Trained
The child was correct. It was a mail train!

Wonderful Walk
During his walk in the woods, the man picked up several burrs on his clothes. When he returned home, he examined them under his microscope and discovered the mechanism whereby they stick on. He went on to invent Velcro.

The World's Most Expensive Car
The most expensive car was the moon buggy used by astronauts to explore the moon. It was left there. Although NASA would like to sell it, no one can retrieve it!

Would You Believe It?
The second person was underwater, so the block floated up. The third person was on a space station, where there was no gravity, so when the block was released it floated unsupported.

Wally Test Answers

Test I
1. Because it has more geese in it!
2. Because they all have telephone lines!
3. So that he can fit in the small spaceship.
4. Exactly where you left him!
5. One. It takes many bricks to build the house but only one brick to complete it.
6. Take away his credit cards!
7. Edam is "made" backward.
8. A mailman.
9. Wet.
10. Take away their chairs.

Test II
1. Lemon-aid
2. A lid.
3. The lion.
4. His horse was called "yet."
5. Get someone else to break the shell.
6. Because he was dead.
7. They use rope.
8. If they lifted up that leg, they would fall over.
9. Wintertime.
10. It wooden go!

Rate your score on the following scale:

Number Correct	Rating
8 to 10	WALLY Whiz
6 to 7	Smart Aleck
3 to 5	WALLY
0 to 2	Ultra-WALLY

About the Authors

PAUL SLOANE was born in Scotland. He studied engineering at Cambridge University and works in software marketing. His passion for lateral puzzles started when he met a dwarf standing on a block of ice in an elevator. His first book, *Lateral Thinking Puzzlers*, was published by Sterling in 1991, and has gone on to become a bestseller. It has been translated into many languages.

Following its success, he established himself as the leading expert in this kind of conundrum. He runs the lateral thinking puzzle forum at http://www.lateralpuzzles.com, which you are welcome to visit. He is an acclaimed speaker on lateral thinking in business. He lives with his wife, Ann, in Surrey, England, where he annoys the neighbors with his hobby as a keyboard player in a rock band.

DES MACHALE was born in County Mayo, Ireland, and is Associate Professor of Mathematics at University College in Cork. He and his wife, Anne, have five children. The author of over 40 books, including one on the John Ford cult film *The Quiet Man* and another on George Boole of Boolean algebra fame, Des MacHale has many interests. He has a large collection of crystals, minerals, rocks, and fossils; he was chairman of the International Conference on Humor in 1985; and his hobbies include broadcasting, film, photography, and numismatics. He is the author of the *Wit* series of books, five volumes that he modestly describes as the world's greatest collection of witty quotes.

Following a chance meeting between Paul Sloane and Des MacHale in 1991, the two have written eight popular books of lateral thinking puzzles, all published by Sterling.

Index

Page key:
puzzle, *clues*, **answer**

Lateral Thinking Puzzle Books
by Paul Sloane and Des MacHale

••

Lateral Thinking Puzzlers
Paul Sloane, 1991
0-8069-8227-6

Challenging Lateral Thinking Puzzles
Paul Sloane & Des MacHale, 1993
0-8069-8671-9

Great Lateral Thinking Puzzles
Paul Sloane & Des MacHale, 1994
0-8069-0553-0

Test Your Lateral Thinking IQ
Paul Sloane, 1994
0-8069-0684-7

Improve Your Lateral Thinking: Puzzles to Challenge Your Mind
Paul Sloane & Des MacHale, 1995
0-8069-1374-6

Intriguing Lateral Thinking Puzzles
Paul Sloane & Des MacHale, 1996
0-8069-4252-5

Perplexing Lateral Thinking Puzzles
Paul Sloane & Des MacHale, 1997
0-8069-9769-2

Ingenious Lateral Thinking Puzzles
Paul Sloane & Des MacHale, 1998
0-8069-6259-3

Tricky Lateral Thinking Puzzles
Paul Sloane & Des MacHale, 1999
0-8069-1248-0

Super Lateral Thinking Puzzles
Paul Sloane & Des MacHale, 2000
0-8069-4470-6

••

Ask for them wherever books are sold.